Meredith Nicholson

PERFECTION LEARNING®

Measuring

Vijaya Khisty Bodach

Table of Contents

1 Using Measurement

How heavy are you? How tall are you? How fast can you run? You can use measurement to find out.

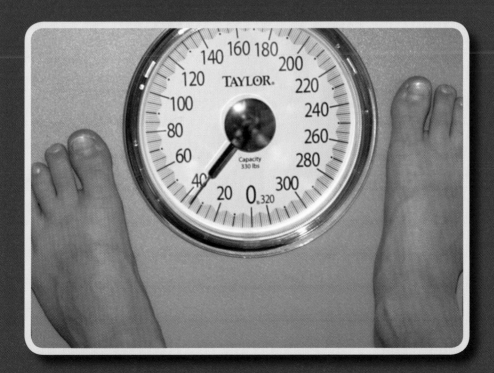

2 Measuring Weight

How heavy are you? You can use a seesaw to compare your weight with your friend's weight. If you're heavier than your friend sitting at the other end, you'll stay down.

If you're lighter than your best friend, you'll go up.

Maybe you weigh the same. Have a fun time going up and down!

The seesaw won't tell you how much
you weigh. You'll have to use a scale. How
many pounds do you weigh?

Do you use a
scale to measure
the fruit you buy?

7

3 Measuring Height

How tall are you? Stand against a wall.
Mark your height on the wall with a pencil.

How many hand lengths is your height? Is the number different if your mother uses her hands? Use a tape measure. How tall are you in feet and inches?

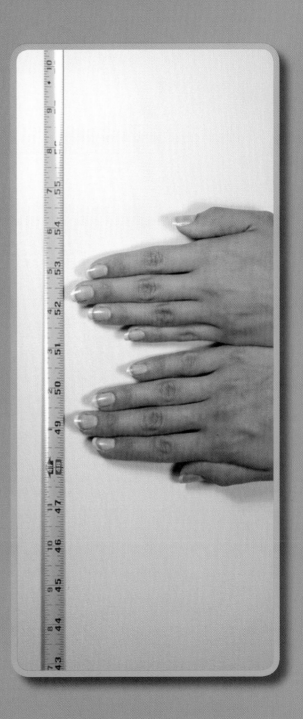

4

Measuring Speed

How fast can you run around the block? Use a stopwatch to measure how long it takes in minutes and seconds.

The next time you are in a car, look at the speedometer. It tells you how fast you are going in miles per hour.

5 Measuring Volume

You may get thirsty after running around the block. How many cups of water do you drink?

Would you like milk instead? Is your milk in a quart container or a one-gallon container?

6 Measuring Temperature

The milk in the refrigerator is cold. Find out how cold it is by using a thermometer. Is the temperature above or below 32° F?

Measuring is fun and useful. You can find out about yourself and the world.

Glossary

Height

Volume

Speed

Weight

Temperature

16

Discovering Science

Leveled content-area science books in Earth/Space Science, Life Science, Math in Science, Physical Science, Science and Technology, and Science as Inquiry for emergent, early, and fluent readers

Measuring
Written by Vijaya Khisty Bodach

Text © 2006 by Perfection Learning® Corporation

For information, contact

Perfection Learning® Corporation

1000 North Second Avenue, P.O. Box 500
Logan, Iowa 51546-0500.
Phone: 1-800-831-4190
Fax: 1-800-543-2745

perfectionlearning.com

PB ISBN 0-7891-6726-3

1 2 3 4 5 6 BA 10 09 08 07 06 05

Book Design: Susan F. Cornelison and Emily J. Greazel

Image credits:

Banana Stock Royalty-Free: p. 12 (right); ©iStock International Inc.: pp. 4, 5; Perfection Learning: p. 9; Photos.com: pp. 10 (background), 12 (left); Susan F. Cornelison: cover, pp. 2, 3, 6, 7, 8, 10 (foreground), 11, 13, 14, 15, 16